D1605694

Teen Tips for College and Career Success

Learn Why 10 C's are Better
Than All A's or APs

Lee Binz,

The HomeScholar

First Printing, 2019

Printed in the United States of America

Cover Design by Robin Montoya
Edited by Kimberly Charron

ISBN: 9781797655352

Teen Tips for College and Career Success

Learn Why 10 C's are Better Than All A's or APs

What are
Coffee Break Books?

Teen Tips for College and Career Success is part of The HomeScholar's Coffee Break Book series.

Designed especially for readers who don't want to spend hours and hours reading a 400-page book on homeschooling high school, each book combines Lee's practical and friendly approach with detailed, but easy-to-digest information, perfect to read over a cup of coffee at your favorite coffee shop!

Never overwhelming, always accessible and manageable, each book in the series will give parents the tools they need to tackle the tasks of homeschooling high school, one warm sip at a time.

Everything about these Coffee Break Books is designed to suggest simplicity, ease, and comfort — from the size (fits in a purse), to the font and paragraph length (easy on the eyes), to the price (the same as a Starbucks Venti Triple Caramel Macchiato). Unlike a fancy coffee drink, however, these books are guilt-free pleasures you will want to enjoy again and again!

Table of Contents

Introduction

Dear Homeschool Student,

Hi there. My name is Lee and usually I write books for your parents. My mission is to help them homeschool you successfully through high school. I've written over 35 books covering almost every topic and challenge homeschool parents might face. This book is different because it's written for you!

College and career success require your full participation and cooperation. In this book, I'll explain the college admission process. Then I'll show you how college admission, college scholarships, job offers, and future customers rely on you mastering important skills for success. So, pay close attention.

Listen, if you are starting out and feeling scared or overwhelmed, I understand! I've been there! I've done this myself and also helped others successfully master these skills. They don't develop overnight — I worked hard for many years. So, you need to start learning them now.

I've collected the best tips from my own experience as a student, parent, employee, and as a consultant who has helped thousands of families (like yours) achieve their dreams.

For this project, I also had a secret weapon — my husband.

You see, before he came to work full-time for me, he was the senior manager responsible for recruiting and development of engineering talent for the world's premier airplane manufacturer (the one that rhymes with *rowing*). He has a unique perspective on what it takes to succeed in the workplace. The core concepts in this book arose from his experiences, both positive and negative, helping young engineering recruits distinguish themselves in their careers.

I split this book into three parts. The first is to help you, the homeschool student, understand the basics of the college launch, including your parents' responsibilities, your responsibilities, and shared responsibilities.

The second part will teach you 10 principles (the 10 C's) of college and career success.

The third part will give you a series of quick tips or checklists to help you through key parts of the college launch.

I hope this book will serve as an orientation for the process you will soon enter and that will continue throughout your college and work career.

Enjoy the ride! I promise it will be a fun one!

Blessings,

Lee Binz, The HomeScholar

Part 1:

5 Fundamentals of the College Launch

Chapter 1

Find a College

First, a simple question (that reveals one of the great truths about human behavior), have you ever changed your mind about what you want to do in your life?

Yes! Of course you have!

Everyone changes their minds about what they want to do when they grow up. This starts with early dreams such as becoming a firefighter, policeman, or astronaut, and can continue later in life, like my husband's and my decision to tackle entrepreneurship in our 40s.

Whether you decide to go to college or career first, your best plan is to get a college prep education in high school. This way, no matter what happens or what direction you choose, you'll be ready.

Be ready for college in case you decide to go. You need a plan in place, a college chosen, and a financial plan. Find a college during high school so you are ready for anything.

Fundamental One – Find a College

There is a sequence of events to help you find a college without pulling your hair out. It starts with a plan for junior year. You can fly by the seat of your pants in high school and can end up with fabulous results if you remember that junior year is the key to success.

During junior year, attend a college fair for an overview of interesting colleges. Ask colleges questions about soccer teams, chess clubs, art majors, or engineering — anything that will help you decide your ultimate (or next) goal in life.

Then you need to coordinate tests. Take the PSAT in October of junior year, so you can qualify for the National Merit Scholarship. Then plan for and take either the SAT or ACT test. Scores might be needed for admission now or five years from now (if you decide to go to college later), or so colleges can decide the first scholarship amounts you receive.

Visit colleges in the spring. It's the only way to make sure you don't accidentally attend one of the top 10 party schools. Remember, merely because a college includes *Christian* in its name does not mean it's a wholesome environment. Only college visits can help you figure this out.

Make a plan for success during junior year. You are unique. What if you want to go to Harvard, West Point, or your neighborhood Christian school? What if you struggle with school and need special accommodations? What do you need for NCAA sports or military careers? You could be living overseas and trying to figure out how to attend college in the U.S. Work out what your special needs and requirements are.

Chapter 2

Pay for College

Fundamental Two — Pay for College

You need to figure out how to pay for college. If your parents have already agreed to pay for your college tuition, it may seem strange that I have included this. But paying for college is one of those shared responsibilities I mentioned earlier. Even if you don't foot the bill, you are responsible to do your best to earn scholarships that will reduce the financial burden. After all, your parents deserve to retire someday and spend your inheritance, right?

To be honest, at your stage in high school, **saving** for college isn't the focus — that ship has sailed. Instead, you need to find a way to pay for college. There are four key ways to pay for college regardless of your savings.

1. Work to win merit scholarships

Don't freak out — merit scholarships aren't only for uber-genius teens, they're for you, too. Not all colleges have Ivy-league standards for giving out merit scholarships. They're based on how you stack up against other applicants.

In addition, merit scholarships are based on your best characteristics, not your worst flaws. You can earn great scholarships by choosing a college wisely and engaging in outside activities and interests. Earn great scholarships by doing well in interviews and at college visits. You can even **ask** for more money, if you do so diplomatically.

Sometimes a college will respond, "Sure, here you go!"

2. Find private scholarships

These require a lot of effort, with writing or projects that only you can complete. By applying, you can learn what scholarship committees are interested in and develop a clear career plan. When applying to private scholarships, you can use the time you spend writing as part (or all) of your English program. You don't have to double up on English credits! You can tell your mom that Lee Binz says it's OK.

Not overdoing English when writing scholarship essays can reduce burnout and give you ownership over the process.

3. Learn how to access need-based scholarships

These are not only reserved for the poor, colleges will take your unique situation into account when doling out the money. So, if a parent is ill or your family runs a small business with a fluctuating income, most colleges understand.

4. Shorten the time you spend in college

Teens can do so through AP exams or CLEP exams. Be sure your chosen college will give you credit for these tests.

You can also take classes at the community college or an online college. This is called dual enrollment and you will get credit twice for each class — once for high school credit and once for college credit. Using these ideas, it's possible to shorten university by one or two years, dramatically reducing the cost.

Be careful, because community college can be a rated R environment. If you and your family are not comfortable with this, have an honest discussion.

There may be classes available at your local community college suitable for all teens, but some are totally off the rails. You can sometimes (but not always) determine this beforehand by asking questions on online community college review sites and forums.

Here is a good rule-of-thumb — if a secular university is not for you, a secular community college probably isn't, either. Your heart and mind are more important than a few college credits, so keep the bigger picture in mind.

I'm sure you want to graduate debt free. At the same time, spending money on a college degree is like buying a car. It has value, it's useful, and it's worth an investment of time, energy, and money.

Chapter 3

Apply to College

Fundamental Three — Apply to College

The next fundamental step is to apply for college. Whether you want to go to college or start a career at once, applying to college makes sense. It's great experience with application forms and interviews, so it's a perfect *trial run* for those going into business.

Applying for college starts on the first day of senior year. You need to work on applications while taking classes and avoid being so busy or overwhelmed that you can't interview well.

Collecting letters of recommendation is part of the college application process. You can't do this years in advance — letters have to be current. They must go directly from the recommender to the college, so you don't even **see** the letters. It's a tough but necessary task.

You also need to prepare homeschool records. These records don't take care of themselves. If your parents don't prepare them, you need to do the job yourself. **Wishing** they were ready won't help you. One big problem is that it's impossible to know which records your college will need, and you need to prepare records in advance. You can't wiggle your nose and presto, they show up!

Get your records ready before senior year starts. Write course descriptions, encourage your parent (your school) to write a cover letter, keep an activity list and reading list, and submit them. You also need to make sure your parent assigns midyear grades in December and final grades after you graduate.

The next step is to complete application forms. Many colleges use the common app, but it's harder to fill out because it tries to fit everybody, which means it fits nobody at all. It asks inexplicable questions for homeschoolers such as, "What is your class rank?" You may apply using the coalition application form instead. And many colleges provide their own application forms. Use these if possible, so your application is more tailored to each college.

Be sure to follow through on all the details. You or your parent need to track your applications and make sure all pieces are completed well before the deadline. For best results, I recommend turning applications in at least one month before the deadline. Once you have turned the applications in, you need to track your results and compare college costs. Figure out how much you can afford, how much debt you are willing to assume, and how to say no to offers that aren't best for you and your family.

Chapter 4

Prepare for Launch

Fundamental Four — Prepare to Launch

The fourth fundamental is to prepare yourself for launch into adulthood. How do you do so?

Understand your goal. You want to become a grown, independent adult, not a cliché (grown child living with your parents). Discuss the options after high school with your parents, whether that's college, community college, career, trade school, entrepreneurship, or military. Have a frank conversation with your parents about boundaries so they won't impede your transition into adulthood (and you won't end up as a couch potato).

Prepare for more than college and career — learn how to become a healthy, thriving adult capable of independent living. Find your calling and choose a career. Many homeschoolers are eager to jump into entrepreneurship, so consider it an option. Either way, make sure you are ready with a resumé, transcript, and diploma.

You deserve a party, so celebrate. This is the fun part! Successful completion of high school is a big deal and well worth a party! This is a significant milestone — you are becoming an adult like a caterpillar becomes a butterfly — a metamorphosis is going on. Throwing a party is one of those parent responsibilities. If necessary, tell Mom or Dad that Lee Binz says they need to start planning!

Chapter 5

Plan to Succeed

Fundamental Five — Plan to Succeed in College or Career

You need a plan to help you prepare for success after high school. Think about it this way, you don't only want to leave home, you also want to **succeed** in college or career.

Learn to be successful in college. You're playing in the big leagues now, where grades matter and networking is important. Listen to sound advice before heading off to college. Know how to get good grades — by reading the syllabus on the first day of class, studying effectively, writing papers, and learning test-taking skills.

You will face challenging times which will give you personal strength and develop character. Don't avoid challenges; you want to learn how to rise above challenges. Talk to your parents about the worldviews you may encounter and listen to what they say about how to keep your values and faith in college.

Let's do a quick self-assessment.

- Are you prepared to find a college that's a perfect fit?

- Do you and your parents have a plan to pay for college?

- Do you have a clear understanding of the application process and are you ready to tackle it?

- Are you ready for launch and feel ready to handle life's next challenge?

- Are you confident in the steps needed to succeed at this launch?

How did you do on your self-assessment?

Are you ready to tackle these five fundamentals of the life launch? Unsure? Don't worry, I will not leave you high and dry. If you need help, the College Launch Solution (CollegeLaunchSolution.com), will give you in-depth and comprehensive training in all five of these fundamentals.

Next, we will dig deeper into the keys of launch success, both for college and for your career after college. This is where I use my business skills to show you how to experience lifelong success. It includes lessons I have been learning about modern marketing, which is much like marketing yourself.

Part 2:

10 C's of College and Career Success

Chapter 6

The Key to Success

Let me start with the number one thing you need to know about college and career.

The key to college and career success is marketing!

You must convince colleges and employers (and customers if you plan to be an entrepreneur) that you are worthy — and you do it by using time-tested marketing strategies

No matter how smart and how talented, no matter how much money you have, you need one important skill — the skill to market yourself.

That's right ... marketing!

Develop marketing skills to attract colleges, job offers, or customers.

- Marketing yourself to colleges — put yourself in front of colleges that are a good fit.
- Marketing yourself to employers — convey your skills and your purpose in life.
- Marketing yourself in business — attract customers who believe and trust you.

Parents - If you have a child you believe in, then it's your job to put your child in front of colleges that are a good fit. You need to market, too. Don't steal your child away from what God intends for them!

Teens – Many people need you to fulfill your purpose. Market yourself to gain the skills you need so you have an impact on as many people as possible.

Marketing includes all the little things you can do to convince colleges and employers that you are real, ready, and right for admission and scholarships. Parents and teens need to work together to make sure you have core classes, a professional and accurate transcript, and course descriptions, so colleges can check your homeschool's academic rigor.

There are things only you can do to convince colleges you are real, ready, and right. Don't be afraid! It's not each college's job to find you. It is your job to find them and properly introduce yourself. Your talents are worthy and important to share. Your calling and purpose are unique.

Do you enjoy ...

- helping friends solve problems?
- recommending movies, music, or books?
- telling stories with your friends?

- having down-to-earth conversations?

If so, you are a marketer! Even as a teen, you are capable of marketing — that's what you are doing in those conversations!

Modern marketing is all about **giving value first**. It is about adding value, inspiring trust, genuinely caring for people, being honest and transparent, and helping colleges make wise decisions about which students are best for their college. Marketing is not slimy or silly, it's helpful! You are helping colleges when you are marketing yourself to them, by helping them find the right fit.

The following are marketing essentials that will help you earn admission and employment.

- Genuine activities and volunteer work — the extra-curriculars that show true interests, clearly demonstrated in a great application or resumé.

- Meaningful college visits — details can be used in the application process.
- Prompt completion of admission forms — these are inflexible deadlines.
- Great letters of recommendation — from someone outside your family
- Self-reflective, technically perfect application essays that seem written by a genuine person — even someone who is still a teenager.

Above all, be genuine

You must listen actively and fully. Be compassionate — empathize and understand what the person wants.

Give generously of your time and effort. Express genuine interest in other people to show you already care. Being genuine shows you can thrive in college and career and will help you make the world a better place.

It's hard, I know; it's hard for me to always be genuine and vulnerable when I'm teaching. I need to share my real feelings and failures to help others compassionately and generously. It's hard to share my failures! But in this book, I am genuinely giving you the concrete tools you will need, out of concern for you.

Earning college and career success is both an art and a science. But once you know these marketing skills, you'll be able to thrive in any college or career.

Colleges and employers want people who...

- are excited to be there
- will stay and succeed
- are willing to work hard
- will make them better

This idea of marketing yourself may be a new thought for you but I promise it will get less intimidating.

Forever Skills

Next, we will talk about the 10 critical C's you will need to know to improve your chances of a great job or awesome college admission and scholarships. The 10 critical C's are *forever skills* you'll use for the rest of your life. We'll go over each one carefully, so you can understand how to use them to increase your chances of college and career success.

These 10 C's are more important than having all A's on your transcript or completing a bunch of AP classes! The A's and APs show one aspect of your education over a small period of time. But the 10 C's reflect the whole of who you are and your character.

The 10 C's could help you become an excellent CEO and COO in the future. Let's jump into these ten keys to college and career success!

Chapter 7

Courage

The first *C* is for Courage — be courageous enough to be vulnerable.

Let yourself be exposed to failure and let people dislike you.

People may criticize you, not understanding your views, the fact you were homeschooled, or even your appearance. Move past fear. You are much stronger than you think.

I'm a registered nurse and I can tell you that adults feel fear. But courage is greater than fear. It allows you to do what you need to, even when you are afraid. When a hospital procedure hurts, people are afraid, but they go ahead with the procedure anyway. You know why? They are afraid but also courageous. They move past the fear.

Courage starts with self-confidence and self-confidence starts with certainty — a sureness in yourself and your purpose. In fact, the more certainty and confidence you have in yourself, the more courage you will have.

You need to have confidence in yourself for a reason. The best reason is that God doesn't make mistakes. Nobody has your special set of skills and abilities, your life experience, or your perspective. There is something unique you are meant to do in this world.

Here's a little insider secret. It doesn't even matter that much if you feel confident. What matters is **acting** confident.

Let me give you an example. As a nurse, I found out quickly that acting confidently was the key — people relax around you and can receive better care when they relax. In fact, if you tense up, it causes more pain and can lengthen a hospital stay. My ability to act confidently was a huge deal, not only for my job but for the health of others. As I became more confident in my ability to act confidently, I could apply it to all other areas of life — teaching and public speaking. I still lack confidence but I strive to act confidently at all times.

There is a lot of truth to the *fake it till you make it* strategy in college and career. Trust me, most adults secretly feel as if they are *faking* confidence.

Chapter 8

Connect

The Second *C* is Connect — you need to connect and empathize with the people you interact with and know how to help.

Connect with people. Practice active listening. Turn off the phone, look people in the eye, and consider what they are saying before formulating a response.

See them, hear them, and truly listen. Try reflecting what they say with "I hear you saying" or "It sounds like..." Show that you understand with a prompt and genuine response

At work, my husband greeted a staffer with "How are you?" and he replied with the utmost sincerity, "Diligent and dedicated, sir!" This was intended to impress but it wasn't genuine, and he didn't listen or hear the tone of my husband's casual question.

Everyone has a problem they want to solve! Employers have many problems. In fact, the underlying question for every job interview is, *"Can this person help us solve our organization's problems?"*

A college's *problem* can be hard to define but a big part is strengthening and spreading their mission. Did you know that every college has a motto or a mission statement? Yup!

At one of the colleges my boys applied, the motto was "Engage the Culture and Change the World." It was all over their marketing materials, brochures, and posters on campus. We knew this college would ask my boys how they would support the college mission. Answering this question was a big part of their application essays and the full-tuition scholarship competition they participated in and won.

Consider how you can learn about the *problem* colleges or employers have. Read their website and brochures. Above all, consider how you can contribute to solving their challenges. Show how you are ready to contribute. The goal of connecting is to stand out from the crowd, not blend in. Connect with universities when you apply. Understand their mission and make sure you support it. Know in your heart how you can advance their mission.

Bring more humanity into your application. Show your connection in application essays. Speak directly with college representatives. Respond quickly and thoughtfully and be genuine.

You need to connect with employers — individuals, not just organizations. Don't merely learn about the company you are applying to, but the specific organization within the company. Learn their mission and unique challenges.

Networking is the key to getting inside information. If you can't network with employees, read trade publications and ask questions before the interview.

Consider how you can contribute to solving their challenges. Bring ideas to an interview. Even if your ideas are imperfect, they will show three things: you are fully present, thoughtful (not only thinking about yourself), and you are ready to contribute.

Follow your interview with a prompt and genuine thank you note. It may be counterintuitive, but email is better for a thank you note because you can use it to ask follow-up questions, give more information, and extend the conversation. These strategies will help keep you top of mind when they make a decision.

Chapter 9

Color

The third *C* is Color — be colorfully unique and authentically you.

To be successful in college and career you need to show integrity. Know who you are. Even if you don't have firm convictions on every topic yet, you need to show openness and reason. Whether you are conservative, liberal, artistic, analytical, enthusiastic, or subdued, let people know who you are.

Don't hide your true self because you don't think people will accept you. Remember how we talked about courage? Prove the courage of your convictions; don't cower in the corner. Integrity is being and showing who you are!

If you are rejected, you will have an experience common to all humanity. Everyone experiences failure and rejection!

All 10 C's are great for both college **and** career success, but think of college as a sprint. Universities look for people who can contribute right away. Prove yourself through your actions. Show leadership in class and within your community.

Your career is a marathon. Employers look for a long-term commitment and proven leadership skills. Prove yourself by solving your immediate supervisor's problems. In your career, avoid flashiness — prove your excellence by your actions.

Avoid cookie-cutter conformity — go out and show your true colors!

Being colorful can compensate for any perceived weaknesses. If you think you aren't smart enough or don't have enough classes or activities, being a genuine and uniquely colorful person can make all the difference.

Chapter 10

Communication

The Fourth *C* is Communication —
you need to show clear communication
in your writing, listening, and speaking.

Be a clear communicator for success and
communicate clearly in these four ways.

1. Communicate clearly in writing — in
    essays, emails, letters, and
    homeschool records.

2. Communicate clearly when speaking
    on the phone or during face-to-face
    interactions such as interviews.
    Speak clearly, avoid verbal tics (ums
    and ahs), and look the person
    directly in the eye when speaking.

3. Communicate clearly who you are. You need clarity when explaining what you stand for and the value you bring.

4. Communicate your vision for yourself and your future clearly. Here's a quick tip. Create an *elevator pitch* for yourself. An elevator pitch is like a business motto or mission statement — short and sweet — quick enough for an elevator ride. I tell people, "I'm Lee Binz and I help parents homeschool high school. I believe parents are capable of providing the best possible education for their children and I provide them with the tools, training, and support they need to do exactly that." It's not only words, it encapsulates who I am and what I do. Create an elevator pitch for yourself.

My husband said an elevator pitch was the tool he used throughout his career to sell ideas to his bosses. Imagine yourself accidentally riding an elevator alone with a vice president. You have 20 seconds to communicate your idea to them and how it would help them solve one of their problems.

To do this, you need to know your audience (colleges or employers) and their issues. For example, for an employer, what are their pain points — their problems (not yours)? For colleges, what is their vision for the college? What are their top priorities for their student body?

You need to know how you or your ideas can help them solve a problem or fulfill their vision. If you can get good at this, you will succeed in every interview because your first words will be strong and to the point. This will make you and your message compelling.

The other part of clear communication is your vocabulary — the language you use to sell yourself. Communicate clearly using your amazing vocabulary to get colleges and employees to pay attention to you. You need compelling words and phrases in your essays, correspondence, and speaking. Vocabulary is how you make them pay attention.

There is a danger in overdoing this. Using compelling language means it needs to come from you, not a thesaurus. There is no bigger turn off than an admission essay or job application sprinkled with artificial jargon or what my husband refers to as "nickel words" (unnecessarily exotic words).

Pro Tip: A strong vocabulary is critical to your personal statement. Work on distilling who you are and what you stand for in your personal statement and try to keep it up-to-date as you evolve over time. If maintained, a strong vocabulary can become the basis for your many future job applications and interview answers.

Chapter 11

Copy

The Fifth *C* is Copy — communicate effectively in writing, using compelling and persuasive language.

Copy means the words you write to communicate what you need to say. Have you heard people talk about *advertising copy*? That's what you are using in your application essays. It's how you get colleges, customers, or employers to pay attention to you. You need to include amazing words and phrases in your essays, speaking, and correspondence.

Perfect college application essays are like advertising copy. Essays should be self-reflective and personal, answering the question, "Who are you?" They should be technically perfect, answering the question, "How well can you write?"

Each essay topic should be unique, and each should touch on a piece of the college's most important question, "Why should we admit you?" Essays should be tailored for each opportunity. Now is the time to be specific.

Your personal statement is the most important thing you will write. If you do a great job distilling who you are and what you stand for (and keep it up-to-date as you evolve), it can become the basis for many of your college applications, future job applications, and interview answers.

Copy doesn't only mean advertising copy. It also means "to duplicate or replicate." You can do this with your application essays. Modify and repurpose application essays you write for one college for a different college. A good example is your personal statement. You don't need to come up with eight unique personal statements if you apply to eight colleges.

This fifth *C* applies to both advertising copy and judicious reuse of what you have already written. You are marketing yourself in words in your essays, and you can copy or reuse your original college application essays — whether applying to college or career. These essays are hard to write, I know, but once you have created compelling, fascinating, engaging essays about yourself, you can **reduce, reuse,** and **recycle** them!

You can reduce the number of essays you need to write by reusing them for multiple college applications and recycling them into new essays that are personalized to each college or scholarship opportunity. Always have an updated personal statement, ready to go.

Avoid self-plagiarism

This isn't the same as self-plagiarism. In college, some students cheat by using the same essay in multiple classes. Throughout your university career, do not copy earlier college writings. With the advent of online plagiarism checking tools, it is especially important to stay within the rules. But it's OK to repurpose application essays, customizing and reusing them for different colleges and scholarships.

Take time to strategize how you will use your college application essays. Choose the best topics from your first-choice college but use prompts from other colleges as well. Use these essays for multiple colleges and scholarship opportunities, and for future job or career applications.

You don't have to be a perfect or even a prolific writer! You only need to do it well for a few essays, edited to perfection. Then you will be able to repurpose them for years to come.

Chapter 12

Content

The Sixth *C* is Content — the content of your education and character.

This C shows who you are. It is the reality behind the marketing *copy*. It includes everything of value you bring to a college and employer. It needs to be included in your application as well.

Show your character in your interactions and your applications. Content includes everything — what you say, your social media, essays, application, and homeschool records. Anything you share with colleges (or what they discover about you), is your content. Learn how to create high-quality content because there is a lot of junk out there (especially on social media). High quality content can make you stand out.

Pro Tip: Look over all your social media posts. Everything you post on social media is forever and colleges and employers are excellent at doing online research to be sure your online posts are appropriate.

You want the content of your application to scream, "This student is well educated and ready for college." The same goes for your essays, social media, conversations, and emails. Each piece of content should build on and reinforce every other piece of content.

Here's an all-too-common example of how easy it is to get your content wrong. Let's suppose Suzy is graduating from high school with great grades, fantastic references, socially conscious essays, and a good sense of humor. Doesn't this sound like a great fit for any career? But what do employers find when they do a cursory search for Suzy on social media? (Spoiler Alert: they always check).

Surprise! It turns out that Suzy is not as genuine as she portrayed herself — she's a party animal who doesn't really care about the values she has shared. Make sure all your content reinforces the message you want to deliver and does not show an inconsistency that destroys your credibility.

Here are some content examples. Each says something about you, who you are, how genuine you are, and your views on life — which show how well you will fit into the career.

Email subject lines — every time you write an email, they see the subject first!

Essay titles — the title should make them want to keep reading.

Content for essays — genuineness is noticeable — using vocabulary you don't really understand will stand out like a sore thumb.

Emails requesting information — written with proper spelling and grammar.

Phone calls to colleges — be professional, take notes so you know what you want to say.

Social media posts — colleges have rejected students because of social media posts, so look closely at them.

Thank you notes — always write them, no excuses.

Cover letters — when sending a cover letter for transcript, records, and activity list, your parent is giving content to the college as well.

Homeschool records — a professional transcript and thorough records with resumé or activity list is critical.

In this short book, I can only give you an outline, but you need to master this area, which is why I hope you'll join me inside my College Launch Solution (www.collegelaunchsolution.com).

Chapter 13

Convince

The Seventh *C* is Convince — you need to convince total strangers to become your biggest fans.

My sons got to know their college admission representative well. He went to bat for our kids, convincing the scholarship committee to give them the biggest scholarships even though they were both homeschooled kids from the same family.

This same scenario happens across the country. Committees get together to discuss the relative merit of each applicant and decide who gets admission or the job. You want someone who will be your biggest fan since you are trying to convince admission reps, employers, or customers to go to bat for you, pick up your banner, and make good things happen.

Convert them through your interactions. Your success is based on the number of actions you take, the number of visits to the college, and interactions by email, in-person, or on the website. Track your interactions and applications.

Write this down ... creating raving fans out of total strangers does **not** require all A's or all AP classes, but it needs effort. You can't slack off, fail to accomplish these critical C's, and expect results. This is not about test scores, it's about having the courage to stand out, connect with people, and be a genuine, colorful, unique individual. It's about clear communication in your writing, personal interaction, and the content of your application. This will convince them to become raving fans.

Chapter 14

Contribute

The Eighth *C* is Contribute — you need to explain the value you will contribute wherever you go.

Make your college applications and interactions about what you can **give**, not what you can **get**. What will you contribute to that college or that job?

Will your presence provide the college with intellectual enrichment? Campus leadership? Passion? Compassion? Humanity?

Will you give your employer integrity? Honesty? Problem-solving? Team building? Skills? Leadership?

Think about the character qualities you can contribute to each college. Don't worry about your weaknesses; go over your strengths — things you love, are passionate about, and excel in.

It's important for others to see your value to the college or to your employer, but you also need to know your value and express it honestly without bragging.

On a separate piece of paper, write down your best character qualities. This will be of great help to you in writing your personal statement.

Think through the following list carefully and talk about these qualities with your parents. They may be a better judge of your strengths than you are. Write down examples from your life that support strengths that apply to you.

- Academics

- Charity

- Commitment

- Compassion

- Courage

- Creativity

- Critical Thinking

- Curiosity

- Determination

- Endurance

- Enthusiasm

- Faith

- Hope

- Humility

- Humor

- Initiative

- Integrity

- Leadership

- Love of Learning

- Motivation

- Persistence

- Questioning

- Resilience

- Resourcefulness

- Responsibility

- Self-awareness

- Self-discipline

- Spirituality

- Spontaneity

- Values

- Work Ethic

Did you write down examples and choose some for your personal statement essay?

This is important because you need to show your value to each college you apply to or to the job you want. Strive to communicate your value clearly. Notice that what you can contribute is not fame or fortune, beauty, or grades. Your contribution is about who you are inside, not what you own. Understanding this will help you succeed in college and career.

Chapter 15

Commit

The Ninth *C* is Commit — commit to the application process.

You need to be committed! Now, I don't mean that your choice of college or career is a commitment like marriage. In fact, that's a common myth that teens believe — that college and career choices are forever. They are **not**! You can transfer to another college next year — you can and will change jobs in future.

In fact, most Americans change their vocation 10 to 15 times in their lifetime. These are not choices like getting married. The choice of college or career is not permanent!

You need to commit to continual research and engagement. I want you to stay engaged during the entire application process. Stay current on what is happening at each college.

How? Watch what they change on their website. Follow and engage on their blog or social media. This is how you get to know the culture of the community. You'll understand what they are about and how they present themselves to the world.

Commit to consistent interaction; this consistency separates amateurs from pros. Here are a few ways you can commit:

- Visit the college online and in-person.

- Read every page of their website (not every college).

- Engage and interact (it's worth the effort).

A consistent personality and tone show authenticity. Don't change your personality or tone each time you talk with them or every time you talk to a different person at each college or job.

One of the most common characteristics among homeschoolers is their ability to interact with people of all ages and stations. One of our church elders was amazed that my 15-year-old son could talk to his peers and then turn around and talk to an older person using the same mature, respectful tone. He was shocked to see this in a teen.

The senior year commitment

You need to commit to hard work in senior year. It's a tough and busy time. It takes hard work and many decisions — including decisions involving money, which are never fun to make! Decide to be in it for the long haul. Once you get through senior year, you can make a real commitment to the world.

Your ability to succeed is so far beyond what you think you can do. My mission is to help you do more than get by or merely get in. It's to help you become both profitable and satisfied after senior year. Senior year is busy for both parents and teens.

Your mission should you choose to accept it

Don't believe you'll have to work hard senior year? Here's an abbreviated list of your tasks:

- find colleges to apply to

- work hard at the application process

- start applications in September (or earlier if you are doing dual enrollment)

- finish essays and fill out forms

- meet and beat all deadlines by at least a month

- engage regularly with your chosen colleges

- fill in any gaps you find (for example, add a missing class or repeat a test)

- apply for scholarships

- fill out the FAFSA so you can get need based scholarships

- visit colleges

- go to requested interviews

- working hard on schoolwork

- continuing activities you enjoy

Whew! You can see why senior year is so busy!

It's not all work and no reward. Full commitment to college and career will change your life — there is no better feeling in the world and success will follow you. There is only one obstacle you will need to overcome.

The millennial cliché

The millennial cliché is that most young people are self-absorbed, always looking for their next job, distracted, and demanding unreasonable salaries, perks, and promotions.

Clichés can be exasperating. It is unfair to paint all millennials with the same broad brush but certain tendencies have become well publicized. Even if these clichés don't hold true, you will need to work to overcome this perception.

You won't face the impact of the millennial cliché in college as much as you will in the workforce. When your environment is homogeneous, age and generational differences won't be as noticeable. But the first time you move into a multi-generational environment — the workforce — watch out!

You will be judged (unfairly) by your superiors because of your age. It's unfortunate, but true.

However, businesses always reward excellence, commitment, passion, hard work, being present at your job, and integrity. They value and seek employees who are *all-in* for their job and their employer.

There is an easy solution. First, be 100 percent committed and fully present at the job you are being paid to do. Turn off your phone to concentrate on the task at hand. Look first to the betterment of the organization and not to your own advancement — this will earn recognition, increased responsibility, and promotions.

Chapter 16

Community

The 10th *C* of College and Career Success is Community — you need a tribe to get you through.

You need to find a community that's a good fit for you — one that will encourage you to grow and become a better person. Avoid a community that will drag you down or lead you in the wrong direction.

Find a community before college

Prioritize finding a community before college begins. This may sound difficult but it isn't as bad as you think. Seek like-minded people who will encourage you.

Look for a college community that shares your values. Campus groups and faith groups (for example, Young Life, CRU, Young Republicans, Habitat for Humanity) are often a good fit.

Network with people going through the application process themselves — the community of other teens and adults applying to college or career. Not many teens (or parents) understand what it takes to apply to colleges. The process challenges you and helps you learn and grow.

If you are looking for a community before college, I encourage you to check out my College Launch Solution. We have a supportive and generous community of homeschoolers willing to support one another and share genuine stories of success and learning.

Find a community during college

One of the worst experiences is feeling as if you are alone at college, with no one to relate to. This is why universities try so hard to promote and encourage community during the first month of a new school year. Take advantage of all the social activities during this time. It can be a time to make new (and often lifelong) friends.

You need others who are going through the same experiences. Here are practical ideas that can help you build a group of friends at college.

Mentor and coach others who are struggling. As well as making friends, you will feel fulfilled when helping others. You will discover that teaching a subject helps you truly master it.

Create or join a study group. Study groups are a fun way to get together with like-minded friends who are facing similar academic challenges. This is how my children met the best friends that they still have today.

Join a faith-based group within the first two to three weeks of school. If you wait, inertia will keep you from joining. Jump in right away so you are settled in a group by the second or third week of school. In addition to finding friendship and fellowship, this will be how you keep and grow your faith in a challenging environment. It will allow you to hold onto your values and ideals. The sad alternative is described in 1 Cor 15:33, "Do not be deceived: 'Bad company corrupts good character.'"

The lessons you learn through building your community will prepare you for a new community in your career. Community is preparation for the team building and problem-solving you will do in your career.

Find a community that fits in your career. Your college community focuses on individual support and encouragement, but your community in your career will focus more on team building and problem-solving. One key step is to join the professional association related to your school major or career direction. My Electrical Engineering son joined the IEEE association in college, the largest technical professional organization for the advancement of technology. It was a great place for him to make friends and network. This can be valuable to career growth and satisfaction.

Finding or creating a community should be one of your first priorities at each stage. You need a community of friends, colleagues, and mentors to achieve your full potential. The friends you make in college and early in your career may be with you longer than you expect!

I hope you understand now why the 10 C's are more important than all A's or APs. Remember, it's not only about how smart or gifted you are, it's about your character and how you present yourself.

Chapter 17

Be a Genuine Jewel

Let me summarize, in case you are totally lost. Be yourself — a genuine jewel, because people of character are like genuine diamonds — they have four characteristics. Like a jeweler rates a diamond by cut, color, clarity, and carat weight, colleges rate you, too.

Cut: hardworking and honest — cut out to be honest.

Color: genuine and unique.

Clarity: clear communicators in writing and speaking and in-person.

Carat Weight: rigorous weighty college prep classes with the best grades you can — your academic preparation.

The world needs your special gifts and talents. Keep going for your dreams. Be genuine and authentic. When you fail, get back up, dust yourself off, and try again like the rest of the adults in the human race. Nobody can do your job except you!

The 10 C's in action

Now that I've given you the 10 C's and explained why they are so important, I want to leave you with a bonus E word — engagement. Engagement is how you will put the 10 C's into action.

In marketing we learn, *"Content is King but engagement is Queen, and the lady rules the house."*

It's like chess. If your king is trapped you lose the game, but the most powerful piece on the board is the queen. Like engagement, this queen rules the house. For college applicants and job seekers, the 10 C's will help you define and demonstrate your character and qualifications. They will see it in your academic preparation, your records, and your resumé. But engagement is how you will present yourself as the answer to the challenge facing your intended college or employer.

For employers and colleges, it's not important how smart, gifted, or beautiful you are, it's important how you prepare, position, and present yourself. Believe in your product (you), and show them what you can offer — your gifts and talents. When you do, you will be recognized and rewarded as the valuable resource you are.

Whether you are working for a company or independently procuring clients as an entrepreneur, the 10 C's matter. The 10 C's matter if you are using these to succeed in your home and family, church or activities, college or on the job.

What do all the 10 C's have in common? It goes back to genuineness!

The world needs your special gifts and talents. Keep going for your dreams. Take a moment and write down, "The world needs me, my special gifts, and my unique talents." Be genuine and authentic. If you fall or fail, welcome to humanity! Do what the rest of us do; get back up, dust yourself off, and try again. Nobody can do your job better than you!

Part 3:

Pro Tips for Teens

Chapter 18

13 Practice Questions for College Interviews

Prepare for a college interview with these 13 practice questions. Look over them with your parents before heading to any college for a visit or an interview with a college representative.

Learn more about how to prepare for a college interview in my article, "How to Win a Scholarship Competition and Ace the Admission Interview" on my website, HomeHighSchoolHelp.com.

Here is a list of important questions and ideas to review before the interview.

1. Why are you interested in this college?
2. What will you contribute to our college community?
3. Which high school courses have you enjoyed the most?
4. What is the most important thing you've learned in high school?
5. How do you define success?
6. What are your strengths and weaknesses?
7. What activities do you enjoy the most?
8. How would you describe your biggest achievement?
9. What is the hardest thing you have ever done?
10. What is your opinion on (current event)?
11. If you could talk to one person (living or dead) who would it be and why?
12. How do you spend your summer?
13. What do you expect to be doing five years from now?

Chapter 19

16 Top Tips for College-bound Teens

Eventually high school ends and you're celebrating graduation. Look forward to the next step with this list of tips for heading off to college.

1. Clean up all social media accounts.
2. Connect with your roommate.
3. Continue applying for scholarships.
4. Get a wellness check-up from your doctor.
5. Go to orientation at college.
6. Find medical services (before you get sick).
7. Use a college packing list (such as my "College Packing List" on my

website).
8. Navigate the college website.
9. Buy and preview your textbooks.
10. Buy supplies (calculators and calendars).
11. Register for the draft.
12. Register to vote.
13. Research clubs and groups you'd like to explore.
14. Set up banking and know how to manage money.
15. Take a tour of your new location.
16. Take placement tests (colleges often use the Accuplacer test).

Discuss details and money-matters with your parents. Don't assume, discuss! Nobody in your family is a mind-reader, so sit down and talk together, adult-to-adult.

Discuss these Topics with Your Parents

1. Will you take a car with you?
2. When can you or should you go home for breaks?
3. How will you get money for living expenses?
4. Do they offer financing or do you need to get a job, or both?
5. Ask for advice about your major, career options, and classes.

Chapter 20

63 Skills to Master Before Leaving Home

One day soon, you will live on your own. You will sink or swim based on the skills you have gained and your ability to adapt as an adult.

This basic checklist of independent living skills will help you find what may still need work. You will leave home with or without these skills but life will be much happier if you master them.

Do an honest self-assessment of your skills. If you are lacking in an area, please talk to your parents about quickly developing that skill.

Live Independently

1. Make breakfast, lunch, and dinner
2. Wake up on time
3. Do laundry - iron clothes
4. Make the bed
5. Clean a bathroom
6. Clean a house
7. Unclog a toilet
8. Kill unwanted bugs
9. Pack a suitcase
10. Go grocery shopping
11. Change a smoke detector battery
12. Take care of belongings
13. Identify spiritual beliefs

Social skills

14. Order at a restaurant
15. Calculate a tip
16. Plan a date or outing
17. Be sexually responsible
18. Be assertive
19. Help others
20. Advocate for those who can't help themselves

21. Maintain healthy relationships
22. Vote

Transportation

23. Pump gas
24. Take public transportation
25. Change a tire
26. Call a taxi, shuttle, or other transportation
27. Talk to strangers
28. Drive safely
29. Water safety
30. Use a map

Finances

31. Pay bills
32. Create a budget
33. Balance a checkbook
34. Live on a fixed budget
35. Track spending
36. Pay taxes

Education

37. Monitor school grades
38. Keep track of assignments
39. Register for classes
40. Navigate to classes
41. Take notes
42. Write an essay
43. Create an outline
44. Speak before a group of people
45. Create a daily schedule
46. How to handle failure

Business

47. Keep a calendar
48. Address an envelope
49. Write a check
50. Back up a computer
51. Take care of belongings
52. Organize passwords

Employment

53. Write a resumé
54. Write a cover letter
55. Write thank you notes

56. How to find a job

Health and Safety

57. Know your medical history
58. Understand basic nutrition
59. Understand the need for sleep
60. Understand basic fitness
61. Make and keep medical appointments
62. Master situational awareness
63. Be prepared for emergencies

Afterword

Who is Lee Binz and What Can She Do for Me?

Number one best-selling homeschool author, Lee Binz is The HomeScholar. Her mission is "helping parents homeschool high school." Lee and her husband Matt homeschooled their two boys, Kevin and Alex, from elementary through high school.

Upon graduation, both boys received four-year, full-tuition scholarships from their first-choice university. This enables Lee to pursue her dream job — helping parents homeschool their teens through high school.

On The HomeScholar website, parents will find great products for creating homeschool transcripts and comprehensive records to help you amaze and impress colleges. And the College Launch Solution gives you all the training, support, and encouragement you need to launch into college and life successfully, without paying for expensive college coaching.

Over the last 10 years, Lee's been the go-to-gal for homeschooling high school. Thousands of parents across the globe have enjoyed her gentle wisdom and a guiding hand as they navigate the upper grades.

The College Launch Solution (www.CollegeLaunchSolution.com) is like having a college coach come alongside. Not just any college coach, though, but one who specializes in the challenges and concerns of homeschoolers! You'll love having someone in your corner who can show you how to find and interpret college admission requirements, explain the changing attitudes toward homeschooling and how to leverage those to your advantage, advise your search for a *perfect fit* university, and teach you how to interact with college admissions staff.

Find out why Andrew Pudewa, Founder of the Institute for Excellence in Writing says, "Lee Binz knows how to navigate this often confusing and frustrating labyrinth better than anyone."

You can find Lee online at:

www.HomeHighSchoolHelp.com

If this book has been helpful, could you please take a minute to write us a quick review on Amazon?

Thank you!

Testimonials

Our whole family is gaining the confidence to launch our children into college and beyond

The College Launch Solution is a great resource!!! It is absolutely what I was hoping for! I felt like we had just an OK handle on all that we needed to do to help our children graduate and be ready for college. But now, I KNOW we can do it with your help!!

I've already worked my way through the first three modules! I have a rising senior and want to use this summer to glean all I can from it. I love the fact that I do have access for 2 years, though, because I also have a rising sophomore, so I know I will keep coming back to it!

I have always enjoyed your webinars, as each one is full of such helpful information. They have given me so much confidence in knowing I COULD homeschool high school. Now, with the College Launch Solution, I feel our whole family is gaining the confidence to launch our children into college and beyond.

My daughter had a mini freak out just a couple of weeks before the College Launch Solution came out as she was looking ahead to her senior year. All of it was a bit overwhelming to her. After she attended the College Admission Seminar for Teens, she was so much more calm and confident. She said, "Mom, it's just step-by-step. I thought I had to do it all in the first month of next year!

But now I know I can just take it one thing at a time."

My favorite quote from you is, "Keep your five-year plan in mind; to have a happy, healthy, close extended family." I found myself getting bogged down and only thinking about how to get through her senior year and helping her get into college. This quote jolted me into a major perspective shift!! It helped me see (and quite frankly, remember) that college is not life! It is just one of the steps leading to success as an adult.

I have also really loved the "extras" you include. Not the major bonuses, although those are terrific! But I'm talking about things like all the handouts with nice, neat outlines, the Year-by-Year Prep Plans, the Guide to College Costs, the College Application Tracker. Real practical stuff that helps keep me organized!!!

I am a very organized person by nature, and before the College Launch Solution, I keep searching for things like this. I found a few items, but **having it all in one place really speaks deeply to my organizer's heart!!!** THANK YOU!!!

~ Johanna in Nebraska

Lee's coaching was worth its weight in gold!

I couldn't have done it without Lee's support and advice! My son was admitted to every college where he applied, was invited to compete for a full scholarship at 5 separate colleges. Lee's expertise enabled me to avoid the college coaches that charge an exorbitant amount of money to do the same thing! My son is giddy with joy, excited, and at total peace. Lee's coaching in college preparation was worth its weight in gold!

~ Kari in California

For more information about my **College Launch Solution,** go to:

www.CollegeLaunchSolution.com

Also From
The HomeScholar...

- The HomeScholar Guide to College Admission and Scholarships: Homeschool Secrets to Getting Ready, Getting in and Getting Paid (Book and Kindle Book)

- Setting the Records Straight: How to Craft Homeschool Transcripts and Course Descriptions for College Admission and Scholarships (Book and Kindle Book)

- TechnoLogic: How to Set Logical Technology Boundaries and Stop the Zombie Apocalypse

- Finding the Faith to Homeschool High School

- Total Transcript Solution (Online Training, Tools and Templates)

- Comprehensive Record Solution (Online Training, Tools and Templates)

- High School Solution (Online Training, Tools, and Support)

- College Launch Solution (Online Training, Tools, and Support)

- Gold Care Club (Comprehensive Online Support and Training)

- Silver Training Club (Online Training)

- Parent Training (Online Training)

- The HomeScholar Bookshelf (Collection of Print Books

The HomeScholar Coffee Break Books Released or Coming Soon on Kindle and Paperback:

- Delight Directed Learning: Guiding Your Homeschooler Toward Passionate Learning

- Creating Transcripts for Your Unique Child: Help Your Homeschool Graduate Stand Out from the Crowd

- Beyond Academics: Preparation for College and for Life

- Planning High School Courses: Charting the Course Toward High School Graduation

- Graduate Your Homeschooler in Style: Make Your Homeschool Graduation Memorable

- Keys to High School Success: Get Your Homeschool High School Started Right!

- Getting the Most Out of Your Homeschool This Summer: Learning just for the Fun of it!

- Finding a College: A Homeschooler's Guide to Finding a Perfect Fit

- College Scholarships for High School Credit: Learn and Earn with This Two-for-One Strategy!

- College Admission Policies Demystified: Understanding Homeschool Requirements for Getting In

- A Higher Calling: Homeschooling High School for Harried Husbands (by Matt Binz, Mr. HomeScholar)

- Gifted Education Strategies for Every Child: Homeschool Secrets for Success

- College Application Essays: A Primer for Parents

- Creating Homeschool Balance: Find Harmony Between Type A and Type Zzz...

- Homeschooling the Holidays: Sanity Saving Strategies and Gift Giving Ideas

- Your Goals this Year: A Year by Year Guide to Homeschooling High School

- Making the Grades: A Grouch-Free Guide to Homeschool Grading

- High School Testing: Knowledge That Saves Money

- Getting the BIG Scholarships: Learn Expert Secrets for Winning College Cash!

- Easy English for Simple Homeschooling: How to Teach, Assess and Document High School English

- Scheduling — The Secret to Homeschool Sanity: Plan You Way Back to Mental Health

- Junior Year is the Key to High School Success: How to Unlock the Gate to Graduation and Beyond

- Upper Echelon Education: How to Gain Admission to Elite Universities

- How to Homeschool College: Save Time, Reduce Stress and Eliminate Debt

- Homeschool Curriculum That's Effective and Fun: Avoid the Crummy Curriculum Hall of Shame!

- Comprehensive Homeschool Records: Put Your Best Foot Forward to Win College Admission and Scholarships

- Options After High School: Steps to Success for College or Career

- How to Homeschool 9th and 10th Grade: Simple Steps for Starting Strong!

- Senior Year Step-by-Step: Simple Instructions for Busy Homeschool Parents

- How to Homeschool Independently: Do-it-Yourself Secrets to Rekindle the Love of Learning

- High School Math the Easy Way: Simple Strategies for Homeschool Parents in Over Their Heads

- Homeschooling Middle School with Powerful Purpose: How to Successfully Navigate 6th through 8th Grade

- Simple Science for Homeschooling High School: Because Teaching Science isn't Rocket Science!

- How to Be Your Child's Best College Coach: Strategies for Success Using Teens You'll Find Lying Around the House

Would you like to be notified when we offer the next Coffee Break Books for FREE during our Kindle promotion days? If so, leave your name and email below and we will send you a reminder.

HomeHighSchoolHelp.com/
freekindlebook

Visit my Amazon Author Page!
amazon.com/author/leebinz

Made in the USA
Columbia, SC
24 January 2022

54109587R00074